Stones

A Collection of Poems

Irene Sipos

ISBN: 978-1-7324191-0-0

Stones/Sipos-1st ed.

1. Poems. 2. Poetry. 3. Verse.
4. D'Amico 5. Female Perspective

NFB Publishing/Amelia Press
<<<>>>
119 Dorchester Road
Buffalo, New York 14213
For more information please visit
nfbpublishing.com

For my beloved family...
with particular gratitude to my husband David for his insightful editing.

Contents

Morning Poem

It is 8 a.m. My husband is in the bathtub
saying *Good evening ladies and gentlemen.*

My ten-month-old grandson is standing at the beaded
chair touching its pearls and stones, saying, *hahhah, go, woof, woof.*

The dog is pulling one toy after another from his basket, growling
to protect against aggressors going for his rawhide or stuffed hedgehog.

My daughter is speaking rapidly about plans that include
an afternoon walk and a surprise that I'm in on.

Namaste, Namaste, Shalom and Good Morning dear day,
I celebrate you and all the languages you speak.

Dog Sitting

You miss your people.
I miss mine.

Your big black head nudging
my hand under the cover as I try

to sleep in the small guest room.
Eyes pleading, tail wagging,

it's only 5 a.m. We are friends, not besties,
not family, together by circumstance.

We walk downstairs, I give you water and
dry food, one pill. I open the back door.

You seek comfort under your particular
azalea bush. I in my borrowed library book.

Election 2016

I

Maple leaves flutter gold, pin oak leaves
shimmer red, sun shines brightly, Bekah exclaims
that the air has turned iridescent pink.

At the corner we greet our friend and her daughter,
walking on their way to vote at the Unitarian church.
They wear borrowed pantsuits too big, floppy, at first

we don't get it, then we laugh. We also voted with
confidence this morning for our first woman president.
We hug and wish each other well. By nightfall our

optimism is slipping. Through the evening we worry
more, we wait anxiously for the final count at 3 a.m.
Next morning we startle awake from the nightmare that has just begun.

II

I lit three candles
in glass jars inviting fire.
The past is never dead

said Faulkner, *it's not even past.*
We carry the weight and we repeat
mistakes: as a poster held high at

the Women's March on Washington
read *My arms are tired from holding
this sign since the seventies.*

Sea salt & ginger, frosted snow, balsam
& cedar, I like diversity even in candles
whose gentle glow brings a memory of the

small fireplace in our carriage house 1977
which was framed by a mysterious fresco.
Vines dripped from the ceiling, owls and snakes

peered out from brown entangled branches.
The artist, we were told, had studied in Florence.
No heat or electricity, the blaze from this fire

warmed us through the famous blizzard. We
concocted cowboy chili on the hearth where
we later curled up in sleeping bags, dreaming,

as wind howled and embers crackled, of the
progress we believed to be unfolding in our time,
finally, toward social equality and peaceful compassion.

Forty years ago, dear marchers, what did we know?

No More

No more nature poems my husband says,
especially spring poems. No more crocuses pushing
up through hard ground. I don't know whether
to believe him. I am shocked and laughing
but he says he isn't kidding. Perhaps he would like

a poem about a couple from Queens who hail a
taxi in Manhattan and discover it's the Cash
Cab. They win 900 dollars which could mean a major
night on the town, although they were considering
casual Greek, souvlaki and salad, or sitting at a little
counter in a noodle joint watching the cook stir fry.

Now the driver asks, *how about double or nothing,*
and they have to decide, like the mud-crusted robin
outside my window, rootlet in her beak, wondering
whether to build a nest in the large-leaved linden
or the slender branches of the silver maple.

First Snow

First snow falling lightly, stubbles
of grass poking through layer of white.
The yard a lathered beard before a shave.

Paw prints revealing paths of rabbits or
outdoor cats whose early morning travels
we otherwise would not have realized.

Inside, football on tv, sound off, players
sliding in the snowy stadium, they punt and
block to a violin concerto trembling from our

speakers. Kitchen windows steam as water
boils in the black pot in advance of immersion
of small shells. I check instructions as this

recipe is new to me. Dave is swearing about our
team's losing streak while he adjusts dampers on
the 1890 Steinway upright he is restoring.

Across the yard, the baby, our grandson,
lunches in a high chair, for the first time,
exploring taste of buttery avocado.

December, the close of a calendar year,
a new cycle will follow this rotation, now
ending quietly, first snow falling lightly.

Never Was

Never was a Star Wars fan, never played
a video game, never understood transformers,

out of the loop with avatars, lasers, comic books.
Not an enthusiast of sweeping allegory, dramatic

symbolism or poetry heavily referenced with classical
allusion. Unfolding the small story, the quiet narrative

has always spoken to me, a tiny window that slowly opens
to reveal. But this year it's all fantasy and fairy tale, masks

and facades, smoke and mirrors, missiles, holograms,
shooting fire, vaulting mountains, storming seas.

We are winning: ending fixed definition, binary
classification of race, gender, relationships, identity.

We are losing: xenophobia, exclusion,
epic threats to Earth and humanity.

Gods and Goddesses, warriors and conquerors,
forces of Good and Evil,

it's TV
it's fable
it's mythology
it's science fiction
it's truth stranger than fiction
it's the morning paper with a mug of coffee.

Different

When you were eight
and you lived on a big, black rock
alone and a door opened
and your father fell
down the cellar stairs and
the nuns scolded with their
fingers flying in your face
and ghosts slept under your
covers and your mother was
confounded by what you couldn't do
and what she had to do and
you knelt on the wooden
floor and shivered and your
heart beat loudly so loudly
the neighbors heard it
booming heard the reverberation
through the window panes but
they couldn't listen, they had to leave for
work and you wanted to close
your eyes, you couldn't sleep,
you had to keep your vigil.

Sunday Afternoon

Uncle Ike and Aunt Bessie sit in our living room
on walnut Victorian chairs flanking the green marble
fireplace. Uncle Ike's Parkinson-afflicted hand in his
pocket will soon press a quarter into my eight-year-old
palm. Aunt Bessie's quivery voice sounds like a pocket
book lining separating at the seams.

Uncle Ike is a great uncle, one of my grandmother's six
brothers, including Uncle Harry, blind and living in the Jewish
Home, his intellect not in league with the others. When Uncle
Harry was a boy he ran away to join a circus. Today, red and
white cane by his side, he is asking if my father would adjust
his radio when he takes him back to The Home.

Uncle Ben lives in Cincinnati. He is the twin of my mother's
mother, Rebecca, who lives with us. She is in the kitchen,
assembling cheese blintzes. The storied other brothers, Isadore
who walked through rooms conducting musical scores, Billy who
travelled to Europe and sent an marble sculpture to my mother in
1918 when she was three (did he imagine it might please her as
much as a soft baby doll?), are gone and entitled to special status
in my mother's Parthenon.

This is not a particular Sunday, it is every Sunday, no one has to
write it down to remember, and no one is ever excused. Except for
my mother's brother, Uncle Paul, who is ill and beloved, and who,
along with his spouse and two fairy-tale pretty daughters, is sometimes
not present, who, too soon will join the mysterious dominion of the
departed, leaving the family in a sinkhole of grief.

17

Poem

Poem of waiting two hours after
school has closed, the six- year-old with
a skinned knee forgotten by the nurse.

Poem of a weeping willow whose leaves drift
into the yard next door, its feathery heaps delighting a child
in the upstairs bedroom looking down, frustrating her father who
needs to rake.

Poem of the innumerable small and complicated parts
of the body that, without being asked, work steadily, silently, in
harmony, almost all the time.

Poem of a voice hesitant to hear itself,
to discover how it might sound, how uninformed
it might be about what others know, how
inadequate its questions might appear.

Poem of quiet rooms that one walks through
when everyone has left, no parents, no children, no
relatives or friendly dog to click-clack nails on the floor.

Poem of the nearly empty # 25 bus riding down
Delaware Avenue at four in the afternoon of New Year's Eve,
proclaiming *Happy Holidays*, icy snow streaking the sky.

Poem of discovering a poem with a line that startles, an image that
reveals, a nervous system that makes us jealous, and a promise
that makes us weep.

A Man Drove to Maine

On summer vacation a man drove to Maine.
Once there he removed his tie.

He sat in a wooden chair looking
over Penobscot Bay. He studied pine
cones scattered on mossy earth.

He listened for loons in breaking water
and awoke each morning to a crimson dawn.

He walked on stony beaches pocketing
pebbles. He tasted tiny wild blueberries
and fresh lobster. He marveled at beach
plums and periwinkle shells.

The ocean rocked the island like an
infant's cradle. The aroma of balsam
fir sweetened the breeze. The susurration
of conifers whispered all day to the man

whose tie, navy with narrow gray
diagonal stripes, lay for three weeks,
forgotten, on the wide-planked
sun-filled bedroom floor.

July 4th

I lay down on top of my bed
trying to find some quiet, ignoring
bits of grit from the dogs' paws that

made the sheets feel grainy. It was seven
in the evening and I was feeling like a worm
wondering if there was a garden up there or if

mud was the whole point. I read some poems
like a diabetic swallowing orange juice. They
were poems about America that I thought I might

use in the summer course I was teaching. I closed
my eyes and the Statue of Liberty said something
in French that I couldn't understand because kids

were yelling and running through sprinklers under
the open window and dogs were barking but I do
think I heard her say, holding onto hope is hard

and it will sometimes break your heart but
get up and get busy because there is work to do.

Secrets

I am not going to tell you about
the time when I was thirty-two or so and
almost died from sulfa poisoning. In the
elevator at the hospital, I saw the white light

and regretted only that I had lived without having
had children and how that epiphany changed my life
and I silently promised I would have children if I
were to live, and I am not going to tell you

about the spectacular double rainbow that materialized
on the way home from my mother's funeral, my older
brother having died just six weeks before, my husband,
daughter and son all gasping through our tears.

I am not going to tell you about how just after my father
died, he quietly appeared at the foot of my bed to offer
a gentle farewell, knowing how sorry I was that when he
slipped away in the night I was not by his side. Visions of

the hereafter and messages from heaven belong in a small book
on a shelf in the airport store which a hurried shopper who
I do not relate to, might purchase as a gift for her mother
before boarding a flight to Palm Springs. Although these

events altered my way of seeing the world and the trajectory
of my life, they may seem fabricated or embarrassingly sentimental
so these moments must remain secrets that I am not going to tell you.

April

April, you are so fecund,
look what you yield,
showers, snowdrops,

fools and babies,
exodus from Egypt,
eggs on the White House lawn,

lilacs, lilies, Earth Day,
miraculous ascent to heaven,
Holocaust Remembrance,

Poetry Month, Library Week,
Buddha's birthday, the fourth
month, the eighth day you
birthed and sheltered me

two months early, April, time
of salt, of sweet, of death, of life,
I am in your mouth,
you are my month.

Tired

Sitting across the aisle
on the B train
I look at the row of weary faces

various shapes, sizes, colors, ages,
a horizontal explication of what it means
to have woken many mornings

to brave routine, to leave concerns at home
along with scattered laundry and unwashed
dishes to head for same/same at work.

I picture each of you, one at a time. I try to
observe without you knowing and suddenly I
see round, soft faces, no creases in foreheads,

no wrinkles like parentheses around eyes, no down-
turned mouths, no slumped shoulders. I see the plump
babies you once were. And with that, a rush of hoping

that you were affectionately held on generous laps, that
you were sung tender songs, that you were offered
a bowl of blueberries as initiation to the messy pleasures

of this world. I hope that occasionally you reach back,
even if only briefly to recall your beginning self as a
visitor new to the planet, unencumbered and dear.

Woodlawn

A small boy
a small house
a small town
on a big Erie
lake with a big
Bethlehem Steel

barefoot
in the garden
tearing tomatoes
from grandma's Hungarian
vines you could
smell

even if the
patched eye
under gauze
and glasses
couldn't see

juicy seeds
dribbling you pull
the radio flyer
to the beach
orange rusty
water bruising
your toes.

Change

A shift occurs after
all these years. The
copper sand on the flat
page of the beach does
not succumb to tidal pull.

The gray-eyed wolf
noses in the snow for
blood. Old rituals do
not make sense.

What is needed now is
precarious as a lone sunfish
in an ancient ocean, relentless
as words that fly from the mind
to their perch on the screen.

Passover

Every year we imagine ourselves trudging
across burning sand, anticipating the next
insurmountable task we will be forced to do.
How thirsty we are, how hungry,

how weary. This year, beautiful pink hydrangeas
grace the Passover table. Deep pink tablecloths
and napkins make us feel we could be at a sweet
sixteen, or in an Audrey Hepburn movie.

If we are not for ourselves, who will be for us?
If we are not for others, who will we be for?

These are the central questions as we labor
under relentless sun, as we submit to cruel
commands of a fierce despot who doesn't care
how young we are, how old, how weak or how sick.

Today we bow our heads against cold
spring sleet, struggling to save ourselves from
corrosive fear and willful ignorance.

Let the crocuses bloom, the daffodils

unfold, the rain fall, let the moon rise
in the blazing desert, let us recline under the covering
of the cool cotton tent, let us recognize around this table
that we are now in the desert 2000 years ago, that

in the desert we were in a northern city in
a house with pink tablecloths and pink napkins
and dear friends. The questions circle us now
as then, exodus everlasting.

Freelance

You wanna know why the sky
is white on an August day. You
wanna know why the wood
fits the way it does, why
there ain't no balance in
this world, no matter how
many times you measure.
Test again with that level
but still it's topplin', all the rich
ones over there, all the hungry
ones over here, the talkers
and the not talkers, the barkin'
dogs and the quiet ones, the men
and the women who want stuff and
don't want stuff and who got too
much time and don't got any.
It's crooked, won't lie down
right. You wanna know where to go
with it, what to do with it, how
do you try, can you transmogrify
with words, with paint, with nails.
The sky is wide open, it's hot, it's white.
The porch is broken, it's unsteady.
The mantelpiece is detaching.
You wanna know why,
why this guy, why.

Wellfleet

Betty and I take off right after Frank's funeral
heading to Cape Cod from Buffalo.

We drive eight hours through light rain.
A rainbow appears, doubles and deepens.

Frank's favorite song comes on the radio. We
text his wife and dedicate the rainbow to him.

Jane comes out to greet us when we arrive
and we decide to swim three bodies of water

in this one afternoon, the pond, the bay, the
ocean. The pattern of tides that ebb and flow

here each day is like the forces that push and
pull across the sea grass and rocky cliffs of who

we are. The moods, the highs and lows that we
sometimes take delight in, sometimes take shelter from.

Memorial Day

Even in second grade it felt insincere
to cross my heart as we stood facing
the flag, knees bumping the sides of my
wooden desk, reciting the pledge.

The terms of the promise I was
making seemed unclear. When it
came to the anthem, what about
bombs bursting in air? I knew

I was glad not to have lived through
that night as proudly we hailed, my
bones would have been quaking in
terror and dread for the other side.

In third grade, my blonde, blue-eyed
boyfriend and I walked to his house
after school. He introduced me to his
mother as she poured milk and offered
club crackers with peanut butter.
My girlfriend is not American, he explained
to her, *she is Jewish*!

In fourth grade, rumors of communism
ricocheted through the neighborhood.
Parents locked doors against children
whose parents wrote plays or made
photographs that asked questions.

What happened to create this pinched paranoia
in brick and stone houses with large leafy
elms, open porches, now empty of conversation?
Children are sent to summer camp,
safer that way, parents meet at private clubs.

On Memorial Day I will remember
the soldiers who have died following
orders. I will honor victory and loss in
meditation and praise and I will pledge
allegiance to an international nation
of those who ask perpetual questions
who, through daily acts of inquiry
and imagination, live in the land
of the free and the brave.

In the Last Century

In the last century I crawled
in bed with my grandmother,
I brushed her soft white hair
and fastened it with tortoise-shell combs.

The quilt on her bed was pale pink
and down-filled. We might have turned on
the radio to hear how much it had snowed
while we whispered about this and that.

For sure we put on slippers and robes and
padded down the hall to sit at the black
and white porcelain table where we sipped
tea from china cups and spooned
sugar cubes from a crystal bowl.

Early morning fugitives, we conspired
to dillydally the morning away. We
might play a game of jacks or gin
rummy before we would go to join
my parents and my brother,
in the busy flat below.

Summer

Fire in the belly
fire in the sky

baby in my arms
summer in my bones

sun in morning sky
sun in evening sky

too hot, too humid
just the way I like it

Earth in Milky Way
Milky Way in universe

blessings in the belly
blessings in the sky.

International Student

You sit next to me in the writing help center,
and apologize for your English. I do not know
one word of your language, not even one letter
of the alphabet.

But you worry about those frustrating articles
a, an, the: sometimes necessary and other times
not. The rules seem illogical. You have spent many
hours preparing this first draft.

As we work together, I am thinking of the warm
country you have travelled from. I am thinking of
the family you must be missing. The flavors, sounds,
customs you have exchanged to test yourself alone

on this campus, thousands of miles from home. You
have questions for me about syntax and structure which
I try to answer. I have questions for you which do not fit
in our thirty-minute session about determination and heart.

College Street

The street is a just a little crooked,
the trees lean too on College Street.

Sitting on a bench outside La Farine
I eavesdrop on a man talking to a friend

about house renovation he and his Korean wife
are undertaking with an Asian sense of design.

Going modern, he says, since the 1920s
details already have been stripped.

Coffee dark and strong,
sun bright and sweet.

Across the street a sign reads
Berkeley City Limit
Nuclear Free Zone.

Dining Room

My parents' dining room was filled with Kittinger furniture.
It was weighty, ornate, carved. When it arrived at our house,
purchased from an estate sale in the neighborhood, I was twelve or so

and wondered why my parents were fantasizing life in an ancient castle.
The mahogany set was foreboding. I didn't want to struggle through
my already intimidating algebra homework on a king's table,

my moods were medieval enough. At dinner, over the years, my older
brother would slam his fists on the table to make a point. No reverberation
issued from this solid surface. It stood its own against political discourse,

family debates. A rectangular matching sideboard was filled with linen
tablecloths, napkins, a silver crumb tray, candles, lace and embroidered
pieces of fabric, all waiting to welcome family and guests who might

assemble to dine, discuss, retell stories. The legs of that table, the heavy
chairs, deep color, breadth and length speak to me now of a stable space
my parents sought as anchor in troublesome times.

Slip Slidin'

Slip Slidin' away
Slip Slidin' away

y' know Paul Simon's
song about the nearer your destination?

Well, he was singin' to me
of my life
slip slidin'
slip slidin' away

as my heart was cracking
in a wailing ambulance
glidin' down the highway

the sky through the back window
so blue

and his voice in my head
so soft

I lay still and rode with the rhythm
whatever my destination

lovin' a sunny September Saturday
lovin' a song
lovin' life
slip slidin' away

Everyone Says I Love You

One hundred fifty species of roses.
More than forty thousand varieties of rice.
Some say the Inuit have ninety words for snow.

I love garlic, I love mail in the mailbox, I love
leopard shoes, and I would love more words to
differentiate kinds when it comes to love.

Poor 4-letter word, too many job descriptions, both
verb and noun, we have so much expectation of you
to express affection for technology, junk food, possessions,
and the preposterous phenomenon of life.

I *loof* Woody Allen when he tells Annie Hall
how much he *lurves* her. I *luff* to listen to Yo Yo Ma,
but not the way I *lurf* a good night's sleep or *leaf* an,
autumn day or *loaf* a crusty fresh baguette.
And not, my darling, the way I *lovitiate* you.

The Way the Light

The way the light, on a 5 degree day like today, the way
it seems to rise from the snow in one instant, like a rheostat
that accidentally gets turned up by someone leaning against

the wall talking with a drink in hand unaware that he has abruptly
flooded the room with unexpected brightness, everyone turns
to look at the sudden shift, it is almost that way when the sun

gallantly illumines what has been steely gray all morning and
afternoon and we now feel as though something essential has been
restored, something we need so much we hesitate to acknowledge

its absence and I wonder if the creatures in their tree branches
and holes and beds under bushes, respond as we do with joy,

and when the light disappears as quickly as it came,
if they too feel chilled and bereft.

Summer 0808

Could the phone
number of my childhood
be sweeter?

A pair of even numbers
that match my birth date,
a prefix that signals long days,
of sunshine, no school.

The phone itself, significant,
weighty, black, sitting on its own
table, ready to connect to
phones in other houses prefixed
RIverside, DElaware, LIncoln, VIctoria

all representing neighborhood, a small
place with kids squeezed between
friends and cousins on porch steps,
one potato
two potato
three potato
four.

Necklace

As a little girl, my mother would show me a delicate
silver filigree necklace that she said her mother's mother
had sent home to family in Buffalo from Palestine, where

at seventy, she had chosen to live out her final days. But to
everyone's amazement, she lived to be ninety-eight. For years
I have worn this necklace and have wondered what color the

tiny inset jewels had been, that except for one, are long since
missing. I have wondered what her unexpectedly long life was like,
where she lived, how, and with whom, and I have wondered what

questions she might have asked God, and how those questions
might now connect to mine, approaching her age, searching
the silence of no one left to tell me more.

Desde la Madrugada Hasta la Manana

In our Saturday Spanish class
Carlos teaches us this word:
madrugada, almost dawn, he says,
that time of night before sunrise.

I love how the syllables scrape,
how they scratch out the slow movement
of unconscious travel when we circle our beds
like Chagall figures in a night sky.

We might be returning from Paris, or meeting
a lost mother at a mahogany dining room table
in a house where we lived many years ago. Or
we might sit in a car, a 1958 two-tone sedan,

negotiating a complicated family situation with
a departed brother. Sometimes it is the one who
has been gone the longest who comes looking to
have a long conversation the way we used to.

We might be outside of Burgos visiting the tomb
of the saint who lies in the monastery
where rosaries were first created: *miraflores*.

Where monks pray in the middle of the night
for dawn, for morning, for a new day
to enter the gray stone walls.

They kneel by simple beds, hands folded, intent,
desde la madrugada hasta la manana.

Dream Houses

The executions were detailed. We labored for hours,
pencil to paper, we barely talked. Homework would wait.
We drew dream houses on big sheets of butcher paper.

I've lived in many houses since.

But none matched the architecture or the furnishings
of those freely rendered with a #2 pencil and
a ten-year-old's unencumbered heart.

Fire Island

That June we drove to Fire Island
with my brother's ashes in
the back seat of our rented car.
Our friend who is a funeral director
and an artist, delivered his ashes
to us the day before.

Blondes were his passion and he
would love coming to us in her embrace
as he would love this trip to the ocean
as a reminder of the best times of his life
which had become dark
and diminished of late.

Next morning, surveying the sand for crabs,
jellyfish and bits of sea glass, we practiced yoga
on the beach, extolled the tide, orchid sunrise,
shells, and tracks of little creatures.

Then we – sister, brother in-law,
nephew, niece – took slow handfuls
from the urn and offered to the sky
motes of ash and dust that spiraled
toward the sun in shimmering ascent
as we praised in turn
and let go.

Hoping Our Grandmothers Found a Way

What did our grandmothers do for yoga?

Not, what did they do to promote yoga, but
when did they get to imagine themselves as
a tree, a star, a warrior, a half moon or a happy baby?

I see my grandmother in her black lace-up shoes,
her neatly belted dress, gold-clasped pocketbook
by her side, in her mid-sixties, as I am now, but

I don't see her nose to earth, her right knee to left
elbow, or both legs up in the air. Did an instruction
book come with age for our grandmothers?

You may stand at the stove or sink and yes, do make yourself
comfortable on the sofa in the den but do not drag a mat
to the floor to pretend you are a downward facing dog.

Maybe the radio on the nightstand, maybe a trip
on a train, maybe the glider on the front porch,
or simply sitting in a pew offered a way.

I wonder, did anyone say to our grandmothers,
This is your time, your body, your breath?

Donkeys

Animals were rummaging
at the back door this morning,
L. emailed from Aruba. *I expected*
to see dogs, she wrote, *but they*
were not dogs, they were wild donkeys.
Isn't life wonderful?

She chooses colored pencils from
a wide bowl on a low table, latte steaming,
screen door ajar to welcome early sun.

Quietly nibbling hay and grasses, the donkeys
assume pastel places in her sketch pad, pleased
to show off their large ears and meditative spirit.

Weeks later, a large flat envelope arrives in the mail.
I take out a drawing of these creatures, who once endangered
in their native country, are now breathing softly in my ear.

Mail

Our mailman comes to the door,
nothing much here, he says
but I see an envelope addressed
to me that contains either
an acceptance or a rejection.

The mailman is a poet who has
won prestigious national awards.
I ask about his new book. At first
he doesn't want to discuss it but
he tells me it is about sleep.

Sometimes he sleeps with lights
on to forget. Sometimes he sleeps in
darkness to remember. He sleeps to
be alone without conversation. He sleeps
to talk to people he can't find in the day.

He wrote a numbers poem with questions:
how are the dead counted in war, how does
the biggest number equal victory?
He says critics claim *my language*
has the sheer force of music.

He shrugs and turns to the next house.
I go inside and tear open the envelope.
My poems are rejected again.

Red

After you filled the sink with blood
we waited in the emergency room.
You lay on a narrow metal
gurney holding my hand
and we named everything red.

Ruby, cherry, tomato,
poppy, rose, cardinal,
holly, ladybug, fireball,
traffic light, valentine, tulip,
poison berry, ketchup, lipstick.

The scarlet tanager, a small bird, male
of the family thraupidae
lights on a frightened branch in
my heart, while you, small bird, female
of my family, listen for the doctor.

Globe

We bought a globe at a bookstore
but did not anticipate that on the ride
home, salt water oceans would slosh
against the car doors, or that the spin
of the earth's axis would make us dizzy,

that we would have to open the windows to try
to catch our breath. I was impressed by how you
kept on driving in spite of the weight of the
tectonic plates as we changed lanes, how you
held lightly to the steering wheel regardless of

the shifting migration of mantles and how calmly
you turned on a classical radio station to take
the edge off negotiating traffic while we were
experiencing the axial tilt of our oblate spheroid
and my excitement in holding the world on my lap.

5 Days 6 Nights in San Juan

Trying to make sense of
how we think and what we do
we travel so far to talk about work.
Coqui sing outside at night,
bananas hang upside down.

Inside, peach marble floors and walls,
black walnut ceilings, enormous Venetian
glass chandeliers, scarlet bromeliad
in tall vases spotlighted from above.
We discuss, listen, question.

At breakfast on a beautiful verandah we take
notes, form small groups, exchange business
cards, use the word *accountability* as we decipher
the government grant process. In the hot afternoon
I read at a table in the pool under an umbrella.

Later I walk down the narrow
beige carpeted corridor on the ninth
floor, past anonymous closed doors dotted
with trays of empty wine glasses, drained
coffee cups, folded newspapers.

In my room, I turn on world news
to hear the anchor report that
President Bush has promised
to *reprimand* soldiers for prisoner
abuse at Abu Ghraib.

Who is accountable? I ask the TV. How,
when, what is *enhanced interrogation technique?*
Reprimand sounds like a minor scold.
How far have we travelled,
all of us, from home?

Three Below and Trying to Miss You Less

How could you have come
for dinner tonight? You couldn't
have. Ice underfoot and frigid air
would have defeated you.

Bundling up, holding on, taking cautious
little steps, the fact that the sun at least
was shining wouldn't have sufficed.
Bitter air would have assailed
your ability to breathe.

I would have made a pot of stew from
a recipe I saw in a magazine that called
for cognac, horseradish, mustard, cremini
mushrooms. You would have called it *different*
and said I didn't need to fuss.

If you were still next door, walking down one flight
and up another would have been too hard, I tell
myself. You could not have come for dinner but
I would have brought you a steaming bowl, we
would have sat and visited, at three below,
we would have sat and visited.

That Guy You Used to Work with at the Bakery

That guy you used to work with at the bakery,
that character who used to get fired and rehired
all the time, who used to call you Miss Elmwood,
stopped me on the street the other day. *Hey, do
you remember me?* He told me he was fired
from the new joint, the really sweet place
that just opened on the water. *A girl's house,*
he said, *I was at a girl's house, and it was stupid.*
He said he's still at the old bakery Tuesday and Thursday
but the new owners, it just ain't the same plus two buses there
and back. He said he lives near the new joint where
he got to eat great food. *Stupid*, he said. He asked where
you are and when I told him Boulder he whistled, *That's far,
she done good!* We shook hands and he said, *If you want
me to read poems for your class, just call me, all right?
I'd be happy to do it Just call me.
Two dollars a poem!*

Mineral Springs

That time Laurie took me to the mineral
springs of Ojo Caliente, we floated
from one geothermal outdoor pool to another.

The Iron Spring said to be beneficial for blood
and the immune system, its giant rock guarding
the place where ancient people of the mesa
received food and water during times of famine.

The Soda Spring providing a sense of calm and relaxation,
its rock walls creating a soft echo. The Arsenic Spring
offering relief from arthritis, ulcers, skin conditions. Each
varying in degrees of cool and warmth.

It was in the Iron Spring, I think, its waters bubbling
from the natural pebble floor, that we looked up at the
immense blue New Mexico sky and saw the likenesses
of our mothers floating in the high puffy clouds.

Was it healing properties from this subterranean
volcanic aquifer that caused us to promise we forgive
and to ask them to forgive us? It has been a long time,
we told our cloud mothers in the sky, it has been years.

We dream of you,
we whispered, we miss you.

Leaves

Oh little girl when you
were my little girl for real
we would go and gather
armfuls of leaves, maples
especially, setting flame

to sidewalks all around us, how
could we resist? We captured them
and brought them home to iron
and press between layers of crinkly
waxed paper to scatter on tables

and tape on windows. Soon they would
crumble and disappear as you, darling, are
not with me today so I must collect yellow,
orange and red beauties to place in an envelope
addressed to you three thousand miles away.

Window at the JCC

There is something poetic about this room
of seniors doing the mambo, the V step, the
grapevine to the front, to the left, to the right

in response to Kathy calling out moves,
encouraging our range of effort, asking if
we are at a 3, 4 or 5 level of activity as we

look out the window behind her. Toddlers
from the early childhood program climb and
run on the jungle gym in the play.

We watch them scramble up and down, one in
pink earmuffs, one in a knitted cap, another
a fleece hoodie, loving a January thaw this

morning after recent frigid temperatures. We work
our bodies and they work theirs, we to renditions
of music we loved back in the day, they to their own

screams and shouts. Glorious for all of us, I think,
as I grasp my ankle and remain in this balance position
of knee pointing to floor for 60 seconds silently timing

myself to the traffic light at the corner behind the kids,
as it turns three times, green, red, yellow, green red,
yellow, green, red, yellow.

Cup

We stir dreams into morning
coffee, silver spoon dissolving black
night. We open suitcases filled with
scrapbooks. We dress with scarves.
The children want paper, paste, ribbon.

The poet reads aloud from his tiny
notebook while we float among wild
grasses and lily ponds. We know you,
we say, your words are under our pillows.
The breaks in your breath echo our questions.

A record player sings. We put down the needle
again. We draw images of the poet in our own
small journals. We wave as he sails past on his
bicycle, we stretch our arms wide and touch
just barely, his free, open hand.

Alpine Adventure

Betsy was skiing in the Alps
with her crush, Rock Hudson, and I
was there too with mine, Rory Calhoun
(does anyone remember Rory Calhoun?)

The ice-crested mountain, a ledge that
jutted past the railing of my back porch,
was so very high and from its peak we would fly
into pure white snow, tongues tasting cold
fresh flakes, sometimes colliding into poplars

that lined the back of the yard, snowsuits and
wool mittens soaked, anticipating steaming
cocoa awaiting us inside the chalet, my
mother making it extra special by floating
white mini-marshmallows on top.

Exodus

There was a road, an exodus, from slavery
in Egypt, so they say, but there was no escape
from the Holocaust, no exodus from genocide.
Only tears to commemorate loss. Year after year,

nations, governments, militias, armies, warlords,
death squads, mobs, secret police, extremists, religious
fanatics, terrorists, executioners, cleanse, exterminate, kill.

European people, African people, Middle Eastern people,
North American people, South American people,
Asian people, young, old, well, sick, people, grieve.

Hands across the city, hands across the country, hands across
the ocean, let us speak out in the city, speak out in the nation,
all the nations of the world, voices across the globe, let us notice,
let us see, let us feel, let us change, let us learn another way.

Used to Be

Us on the dance floor
you with the moves
me loving the whirl
of everyday minutia
dissolving into sound
and motion, brain taking second
place to heart and feet.

Used to be I rocked
the high heels and vintage
dresses, back then fifteen cents
at rummage sales. A glass of wine,
a blast of chords, you in your Chucks,
free stylin', people breaking out laughing.

Don't misunderstand, I'm delighted
to watch you kids now, shiny hair flying
to fast beats, I'm grateful as hell, I'm
having fun, maybe it's just on this cold
night that I'm tapping the floor on the side
lines with warm winter boots, wondering
about getting used to used to be.

A Blue Suit

She wears a blue suit to match her blue eyes,
he wears Army khaki. In the rabbi's study, marriage
vows, 1942. Who sees what lies ahead?

Train to Tampa. She detests Florida forever,
after equating the South with humidity and
discrimination. One two three four five years,
he is stationed in the Philippines operating Morse

Code and sending long-hand letters home. In future
decades, like kids dating, they go out for lunch, for dinner,
they go out to dance, visit friends, tell stories, to be together,
to erase time, distance, fear and war.

Raining in San Juan

The bus cost 25 cents.
It stops outside the iron
gate of the hotel. *Old San Juan
is beautiful*, everyone says, *you
must not leave until you go there.*

The rain is a wall,
there is nothing to see.
Taking refuge in the café,
no jacket, no umbrella, my dress
sticks to my skin.

I have never in my life
seen rain like this, I say.
You have never been in Puerto Rico,
the waiter laughs.

On the way back, the bus sails
by pastel houses, store fronts,
schools, a cemetery. People wave
at the driver.

Water sloshes between the
pedals, down the aisles, under
seats. Exclamations punctuate
the air and now I understand,
the brakes are not working.

At home, although it is May,
there is snow. I want to stay
in this pink city where
the view has disappeared
and the bus has taken flight.

Thirteen

Girl with toothpicks
pinned through dandelions
in her hair, entwined
with tiny pale violets

who wondered at four
if tenderloin behind glass
at the butcher's came from
tender lions

who has lived since ten
on grain and grass, who has
hollering in her heart, who has
screams in her dreams

who sleeps on watch for spiders
and ghosts, who wears shoes ten
feet tall who writes a poem that says
my outfit kicks ass, it kicks many asses
many times.

For Eli

I love how you guys get sweaty,
bounce balls off your heads, kick
farther than far, then farther than
that, send ball to sky, run toward,
run for, swift legs, guys on sideline
tap balls up down, up down, dart back
to field, stick with team, run like hell,
slide shoulder to ground, game over, slap
up, flushed, hot, off to sponsor bar for beer.

Yours 'till Niagara Falls

Little Jill,
we called each other
Queer Beer #1, Queer Beer #2.
Unlike me, you were always adorable,
even your hair obeyed you.

We collected tiny glass
animals to arrange on the kootchie
shelves in our bedrooms.
Saturdays we took the #20 downtown
to order tuna on white with
mayo at the Statler and search in
secondhand bookstores for Salinger and Saroyan.

We shared our fears
of boys, of girls, of confinement,
of freedom, of boredom, of
hysteria, of our bodies.

I stand beside you now,
touching your hand, remembering
root beer barrels, Sugar Daddies, Forever Yours,
cookie dough, all the sweets we shared
and I wonder how you came to
die unexpectedly beside
the mighty Niagara.

Song

A Chinese student in my writing class says
I couldn't hand in final paper, I am sorry.
My grade book makes me press for more
information. *My father dies,* she says.

I go to the funeral to express my sympathy
to her mother. *I am so sorry,* I hug her
although we haven't met before. *My husband,*
we marry forty years, then she says *every night,*

we sing, I lie next to you, you lie next
to me, I picture them, slim and neat in
their bed. She repeats the refrain, her voice lilts.
I lie next to you, you lie next to me.

Winter Journey

A friend texts: *I am standing
in front of the Empire State Building
fat flakes are falling.*

How I wish I were there to see the loveliness
of snow that hushes and slows Manhattan.

In dark January as a kid, I would play Tchaikowsky's
Symphony #1 on the record player in my room, its album
cover, an orange moon against a midnight blue sky.

Snowing now in Buffalo, I put on the melancholic
first movement, *Dreams of a Winter Journey.* As I do,
the musicians take their seats, nod to one another and tune
their instruments in the splendid concert hall, St. Petersburg, 1866.

Wind wails, carriages gently deposit ladies and gentlemen cloaked
and furred, top-hatted and gloved, settling in as the orchestra begins
to evoke the Russian winter of a twenty-year-old genius composer.

And I hear the symphony swirling across New York, winter dreams flying
from ice-covered windows in my living room to Peter on Fifth and West 34th.

Worry

My mother is worried about her cable bill.
My husband is worried about his printer.
I am worried about my sense of humor.
My son is worried about the faucet
he didn't turn off last night.
My daughter is worried about the world.

The mouse in our house is worried
that our traps will catch him and
I am worried that they won't.
One of our dogs is worried about
wanting to open the refrigerator.
The other dog is worried about
other dogs in the neighborhood.

My brother is done worrying but that's because
he died from worrying about our mother
My father is dead also but he is worried
about the mess we're in because he
is the kind of guy who keeps on worrying.

Sunday Blues

They creep up your spine in
elusive little indigo slippers, no,
they do not wear black boots but
the subtle pressure lets you know

they have staying power, they are tough to
ignore. You do try to read the paper, make soup,
take a walk, listen to Stevie Wonder croon
You Are the Sunshine of My Life.

You tell yourself homework anxiety should
have ended long ago. No crushing deadlines
wait on tomorrow's desk. Why then is the solitary
figure sitting in the bus stop shelter outside

the bowling alley or the darkened store window
of the vacuum repair shop more melancholy
tonight than it was yesterday or will be tomorrow?
Even beauty hurts. Dave remembers as a kid

he would hear his father play violin concertos
on Sunday afternoons. He would go to his room
and shut the door, hoping that no one had
caught him trying not to cry.

Stones

I place a small
stone on my father's
marker flat to the ground
to say, your memory lasts
solid and enduring.

I place a small
stone on my father's
marker flat to the ground
to say, rest peacefully
no need to ache and wander.

I place a small
stone on my father's
marker flat to the ground
to say, this pebble, your name,
is carried in God's sling

as long ago the stones of shepherds
tallied with the numbers
of the flock for safe-keeping
across mountain tops. I catch
strains of an ancient song as

I place a small
stone on my father's
marker flat to the ground, that says,
There are men with hearts of stone
and stones with hearts of men.

Poetry

Don't do it because you want
to get something off your chest
it's not about your chest.

It's about what wants to sound
itself out, to skip and slide into
shapes of spaces and swooshes

spoken or broken
in lines
on the page.

Don't do it to shove in a drawer
you have enough stuff in your drawer
don't save it, spend it, send it,

donate it to a pocket,
leave it on a subway seat,
scrawl it on a rock, chalk it on a wall,
don't lock it, don't block it.

Place two poems
in closed fists and offer
this hand
or that.

Cross Country Flight

Ancient poets, I once read, deemed travel as
one of four noble subjects. Walking distances in
sandals, perhaps with a carved bamboo cane, riding
a donkey part of the way, nighttime darkness all around.

How courageous to defy the unknown, to set out for
uncertain adventure, uncharted landscape. And here I am,
cell phone in hand, with light luggage, steel wings, friends
at my destination, yet I need to think of this romantic notion,

to push away prickles of fear before I board the plane. I am
in comradeship with ancient wayfarers in search of profound
experience! Ashamed of my apprehension, I recall the
other themes considered worthy: love, song, and blood.

Oh, these journeys to the interior are old familiars,
I know their pathways well.

Previously Published Works

"No More," The Comstock Review, vol. 29:1, Spring/Summer 2015
"Different," Artvoice, October, 1998; The Buffalo News, September 1998
"Poem," The Buffalo News, December 20, 2015; Just Buffalo Literary
    Center 7th Annual Members' Contest, Spring 2015
"Tired," The Buffalo News, December 18, 2016
"Woodlawn," Broadside, Park Street Press, Fall 2014
"Change," Lilith Magazine vol. 25, no. 3, Fall 2000
"Passover 2004," The Buffalo News, May 2005
"Freelance," A Celebration of Western New York Poets, Buffalo Legacy
    Publications, 2016
"Memorial Day," The Buffalo News, 2010
"Everyone Says I Love You," (in a slightly different version) A
    Celebration of Western New York Poets, Buffalo Legacy
    Publications, 2016
"Desde la Madrugada Hasta la Manana," The Comstock Review, vol. 18,
#2, Fall/Winter 2004; The Buffalo News, September 5, 2004
"Red," The Buffalo News; Earth's Daughters 40th Anniversary Issue #80,
    Perennial Forte, 2011
"Globe," Earth's Daughters, #86, Shift, 2015
"Three Below and Trying to Miss You Less," (in a slightly different
    version) The Buffalo News, Fall 2008
"Cup," The Comstock Review, vol. 29:2 Fall/Winter 2015
"Exodus," The Jewish Journal of Western New York, October 2014
"Used to Be," Earth's Daughters #91, Lines, 2018
"Sunday Blues," Poem… Other Poems, Buffalo Ochre Papers, No.12,
    2017
"Stones," Lilith Magazine vol. 40, no. 3, Fall 2015
"Poetry," The Buffalo News, April, 2010; A Celebration of Western New
    York Poets, Buffalo Legacy Publications, 2016

About the Poet

Irene Sipos earned her Master of Arts in the legendary 1970's English Department of SUNY University at Buffalo. She recently retired from SUNY Buffalo State where she taught in the English Department and the College Writing Program and was a co-founder of Buffalo State's Rooftop Poetry Club.

Her work has appeared in Lilith Magazine, The Comstock Review, Earth's Daughters, Buffalo Poets Against War, Burchfield Penney Newsletter, The Jewish Journal of Western New York, Artvoice, Buffalo News, as a Park Street Press broadside and in the anthology, A Celebration of Western New York Poets. Her chapette, Poem... and other Poems, is No.12 in the Buffalo Ochre Papers. She was a finalist in the 2004 Comstock Review Awards Issue and the 2015 Jesse Bryce Niles Chapbook Contest.

Currently, Irene works at the Writing Center at Buffalo State and is a freelance editor and tutor.

Made in United States
Orlando, FL
27 July 2024